TRAILS OF THOUGHT

A COLLECTION OF POEMS

CRYSTAL DAVID JOHN

INDIA • SINGAPORE • MALAYSIA

Copyright © Crystal David John 2025
All Rights Reserved.

ISBN

Hardcase 979-8-89724-283-2
Paperback 979-8-89556-346-5

*Dedicated to my dearest Parents, Husband, and
Daughter.*

Contents

Preface

The title of my book - *Trails of Thought,* was chosen to symbolize the parallels between the journey of a hiker and those of a thinker. As my thoughts meander through the complexities of life – they often paint a vivid, dull or petrifying picture. The outcome of this often culminates in the composition of a poem, the conclusion of which often is most unexpected. As I traverse the trails of thought, I encounter moments of clarity and confusion, enlightenment and bewilderment. Like a hiker facing unexpected obstacles or breathtaking panoramas, my thoughts lead me to new perspectives and revelations. This journey challenges long-held ideas and childhood beliefs, inviting me to embrace unconventional thoughts. By accepting my unorthodox musings, I embark on an endless exploration of my mind, uncovering the intricate beauty of my consciousness. Each step deepens my self-awareness and understanding of the world, forging a path toward greater insight and discernment.

This book is a collection of such an experience in the form of poems I have written over the past years.

I am deeply thankful for the unwavering love and guidance of my late parents, Abraham N. David and Christobel J. David who instilled in me the value of my own opinion, of determination and attention to details. My late husband, Jacob John Chellaraj, was a pillar of strength and motivation who always urged me to share my poetry with the world, many of which I had composed even before I met him. It goes without any doubt that Crystaline Jeanetta John, my daughter, has always stood by me encouraging and urging me to publish my poems. This little critique has always, in her forthright manner given me constructive feedback, and has thereby played a pivotal role in bringing this book to its final form, in fact she is the one who chose the title of the book.

Compiled over around thirty-five years, the poems in this book intend to offer a unique glimpse into various themes, styles, emotions, and perspectives as they unfolded and evolved in my trails of thought.

I hope these poems take you down your own trails as you set out to read some of mine in this collection of poetry. ☺

Dr. Crystal David John
Chennai

Trails of Thought

As trails of thought unwind
In the labyrinth of my mind,
Twisting, turning, weaving, dreaming,
My poetries start evolving.
The trails amble like a river in my mind,
Creating new paths – not leaving the old behind.
Each trail traces a story of old,
Leading to a poem – new and bold.
Steering through memories of joy and fear,
Some trails are familiar and very clear,
Others are uncharted, winding and free,
The outcome of the poem till the end I cannot see!
Thus, in the trails meandering in my mind,
Beautiful treasures and wonders I finally find!

(05.05.2022)

* * * * *

Abstract Art

Shapes and lines merge into a visual cacophony,
Colours dance around forming a symphony.
Abstract art defies and skirts all rules,
As emotions unfurl in abstract hues.

Expressions unleashed into a graphic storm,
There're no regulations of a distinct form.
Bold strokes, ink drops, chaotic and free -
Throws wide the window to the soul's decree.

This, a simulation of the world around,
In this madness messy beauty is found.
Wrapped emotions emerge to release,
The beautiful canvas, finding inner peace.

So, discover the depths of layers unseen,
Life's a realm where imaginations convene!

(01.10.2023)

* * * * *

Absurdity

Behold the emperor who all revere,
He walks around naked, as his followers cheer,
With every lie he utters they nod and believe,
The idiocy of it all - they fail to perceive!

Watch him as he stands up so bold and bare,
All grades are a sham, but who would care?
For with confidence, he struts along with pride,
As his presence commands attention far and wide!

In this ludicrous era where logic is defied,
Science is but a joke, and reason is cast aside.
Gravity? What's that? when the emperor can fly,
With invisible wings, in the bright blue sky.

The cats and dogs hover – oh yes, they can -
For he says so, waving the rainbow as a fan!
Denying gravity, they navigate around with grace,
The clouds form their streets, in this insane space.

Donkeys fly around in a sky that is not blue,
Their skin so multicoloured – a vibrant hue,
Fish swim in the air, and birds live under the sea,
In this topsy - turvy world, where absurdity runs free!

In the emperor's world, reason has no sway,
The 'laws of nature', defined by him, is here to stay!
In every twist and turn, inanity is in sight,
In this carnival of chaos, surreal delights ignite!

Oh, clap your hands as the emperor looks grand,
Strutting as the symbol of wisdom in every land!
All his followers worship him with blind devotion,
Believing the preposterous, sunk in their delusion.

So let us all carouse in this circuit of deceit,
Where truth and reason sleep in the backseat.
In this realm of mockery, fools are crowned -
And the emperor reigns all naked and renowned!

For there is no honest little boy who would scream,
"The emperor is naked this is real, not a dream!"

(24.11.2023)

* * * * *

A Child's Ear Ring

The ring with elegance and grace,
In sparkling gold finds its place:
Crafted carefully and designed,
With a little flower well aligned.

The petite ring with charm untold,
The tiny flower, with petals unfurled,
Hangs like a little swing so light,
For a fairy to hover, and alight.

Like stars that dance across the sky,
Bringing sparkle to every eye,
A symbol of love and endless grace -
As it decorates this child's face.

A reminder of dreams in flight,
A grandma's gift, a ring so bright.
Personifying many tales
Of her dear love, that never fails!

So let it dance and let it swing,
This delicate pretty little thing,
The golden swing that gently sways,
Bringing joy in its whimsical ways!

(28.09.2021)

* * * * *

A Dark Dot

In a dark dot,
I as a spot,
lie.
As tears I cry
all crouched,
and perched,
in the hollow suffocating,
fists clenching,
as the space around,
caves in, and walls surround
me with spikes, that inward poke,
and the voices that spoke
I heard loud and clear,
and I fear
the laughter
above the clatter
which is nauseating
and revolting,
as into the abyss I slip,
and in the mire dip,
screaming so loud,

but none in the crowd
hear me,
yet see
how I cringe and tremble in fear
as panic hits, I can hear
the deafening silence of the dot
as the spot
comes hurling at me,
driving me into the raging sea
that engulfs me!

And then the light's beam
so freaking bright
that in my dream
I'm blinded by that light,
which splits the dot that held me tight
into a splintering ray
obliterating my day!

(30.04.2021)

* * * * *

A Diamond in Ashes

In the darkness of despair where shadows loom,
Evolves the diamond from the ashy gloom.
From fiery trials and pressured pain,
Emerges the diamond struggling - not in vain.

The cuts and chips make the light shine bright,
Revealing beauty hidden from sight.
The diamond in the ashes formed by the flame,
A witness of resilience it does proclaim.

Each facet carved and every tear shed,
Polishes the diamond and the soul's thread.
Through disdainful despair, hope still thrives
Like the diamond in the furnace, our spirit survives.

For in the deep dangerous dark and doomed night,
The diamond, the survivor – brilliantly beautiful, bold and
bright.

(Written for my niece - Gabriella Sharon David)
(29.07.2019)

* * * * *

A Door

In the realm of options – observe the door,
A gateway of curiosities, an entrance to explore.
As you enter, you'll experience untold tales,
Where the present will bloom, the past will pale.

As you turn the knob sighing with fear,
Do not worry for courage is near.
Unpack the doubts that hold you back,
Walk with confidence on the new track.
Fear no obstacles that may arise,
For they'll be prospects in disguise.

Believe in yourself, and in your power,
For your spirit will blossom like a flower.
Within you lies the passion to aspire,
To chase your dreams and not ever tire.
Grip the door with confidence and grace,
Discovering your purpose in this new place.
Beyond the door lies a version of you,
Which you need to capture and pursue!

Step through the open door, a new chapter will unfold.
Discover the version of you, waiting to be told!

(Written for my daughter – Crystaline Jeanetta John)

(18.09.2023)

* * * * *

A Gem

You, my daughter, a friend for life,
A pillar of constant strength
Against the maddening strife,
You stand by me to any length.
You are sparkling and rare,
A precious priceless gem...
A treasure beyond compare!
And from you will always stem,
Brutally honest emotions and care,
That will shine brightly I know -
Here or there or anywhere,
Like the sunbeams that glow!

Your laughter brings such solace,
In your concern, I find a light,
The tests of time you help me face,
Like a beacon in the darkest night.
Your love and care so open and true,
A bond that time can never sever.
In every moment I see in you
A gem, a gift I'll cherish forever.

In this tapestry of life we weave,
So well interlaced in harmony -
Through all the joys and sadness, I believe
That the love we share is a melodic symphony!

Through every trial and every care,
The highs and lows we together share,
Our bond grows stronger with time,
Like a poem with a perfect rhyme!

(Written for my daughter – Crystaline Jeanetta John)

(23.04.2022)

* * * *

A Letter

Dearest writer,

Use me for a just and right cause,
Let the ink in me never pause,
I am here to help you fight,
With peaceful force and our might,
To see that issues are brought to the light,
So that chaos and corruption is set right.
Yes, reading what I help you write,
Will cause panic and fright,
And for some, extreme delight,
Because together we bring insight!

Your Sincere Friend
Pen

(04.09.1990)

* * * * *

A Letter from Me to You, My Child

I see the tears you have shed,
And the sadness in your eyes,
But please do not be depressed,
For my love for you never dies.

Though I'm not there to pray for you,
Or hug and give you a kiss,
I know my presence in your home,
Is another aspect you'll sorely miss!

Memories will cloud you today,
Filled with joy, sorrow, and love,
But just be happy and realise,
That I'm celebrating in heaven above.

And when sorrow overwhelms you,
Just pray and God will make you strong,

You will then live in His perfect peace,
And remember I'm home, where I belong.

Written on my mother's birthday. I lost her on 18/2/23

(03.09.2023)

* * * *

A Little Mark

It heralds in a pause,
This little innocuous mark,
Giving another insight,
Like a spark illuminating the dark.

With grace it makes you stop,
The flow of a writer's thought,
Allowing the words to breathe,
Sifting ideas, while together they're brought.

A light that brightly shines,
Making sense, the path it clears,
Untying ideas with tact,
The ship of knowledge it prudently steers.

Directs the sea of sense,
With precision clears the way,

Guiding readers through the waves,
The comma, from its duty never sways!

(17.09.2017)

* * * * *

A Morning Prayer

Lord God be with me today,
Help me all along the way.

Give me self-control and love
And patience, Lord, from above.

Through my struggles great and small,
Be with me Lord, my All in All.

I know that I'm in Your care,
And that You have heard my prayer!

(03.05.1987)

* * * * *

Angst

Deep down within a storm does brew,
A relentless wave of angst, crashes through,
Shadows of restless thoughts in the night,
Causing fear's grip to squeeze so tight.

Doubts and qualms – a constant companion,
Thoughts in my dream like an endless canyon,
A tempest of emotions dangerous and deep
Causing an inner turmoil, impeding sleep.

Locks up the doors of peace and serenity,
Blurring all images of visible clarity,
The journey proceeds in uncertain plots,
As the routes mingle into tangled knots.

(07.03.2020)

* * * * *

A Plea

How do I help
when you stay so far?
Do you need me
to help erase the scar?

Beautiful you are,
and so we can be,
let's join hands
to adorn eternity!

Stuck in the cog of life,
may make you miserable,
but the mist will clear
making things visible.

Let me help you heal,
so please let me in,
you are amazing
and there's no discord within.

Together we shall resolve,
together we will win,
together we conquer,
just let me in!

(29.05.2023)

* * * * *

A Poor Mother

In the heat of summer mother is anxious
For water, as the well runs dry.
In winter she is anxious when
In the cold her children cry.
In the monsoon season she worries
When the roof leaks like a sieve,
All year through she agonizes
That her little girls should safely live.

She worries and worries
For getting food on the plate
And about the cash squandered
By her jobless, irresponsible mate.

She worries and worries,
About rice and curries,
About debt and rent,
And all the money spent.

(05.07.1998)

* * * * *

A Treasure

I pine for you every day,
Since you left us on that awful day.
Your prayers kept me safe and warm,
Bringing peace in a life of storm.

The space you left is unfillable,
Your love stretched to infinity,
Your consoling presence often
Was my link to sanity!

I learned to love and forgive from you,
And strength to overcome my fears,
You gave me music, laughter, and fun,
All through my yesteryears.

You fought cancer for three decades
So courageously, all along
Your faith in God was admirable,
Indicating how life's a joyous song.

I have a video taken of you,
With you laughing and joking.
Just ten days before you collapsed,
So full of life – it was shocking!

Remembering you for all you've done,
Gives me so much pleasure,
Every day I thank God above,
For a mother I so treasure!

(Written for Mother's Day)

(14.05.2023)

* * * *

Baa Baa

Baa baa white sheep
have you any wool?
yes sir, yes sir
all bags full,
for the black sheep worked,
all on her own,
while I slept and rested
in my palatial home.

The proletariat, and sidelined.
and the labouring lower caste.
are oppressed and exploited -
forever burdened, forever outcast!

Their bleating unheard -
their struggles unseen -
while the bourgeois,
always reign supreme.

Fully demoralized,
they work in vain,

as the rich get richer
and the deprived, poor remain.

While children recite this rhyme,
teach them every time
to remember the poor's plight
and to rise up for them, and fight.

(07.08.2020)

* * * *

Be Sincere

All candles tall and short,
Whether stout or very slim,
Do but always impart
Light, which is never ever dim.

Watch the roses grow,
They don't mind the thorns.
Seen the lotus glow,
Ne'er the slush it scorns.

So too must we shine,
In our own little way,
For in God's own time
Our actions will repay.

Ne'er be disheartened,
If your contributions seem small.
As burdens are lightened,
By the sincere efforts of all!

(20.04.1986)

* * * * *

Be the Light

Be the wind in someone's sail,
be the calm in someone's gale,
be the spark today,
in someone's dark day.
Be the joy that's found,
turning another's day around.
Be the hope in someone's gloom,
The sunshine - helping flowers bloom.
Be the light in someone's night,
and their breastplate in a fight,
and your kindness, always share
in what you do, and how you care.
Be the reason to make them smile,
even if it is for a little while.
In a world that is so tough,
with a whole lot of toxic stuff -
be the balm - soothing the strife
in someone's stress filled life!

(14.12.2000)

* * * * *

Better Fiends

In the corners of my mind, where shadows creep,
There dwell the fiends that often lie asleep.
But when they awake their whispers are unkind,
And with doubts and fears they torment my mind.

Their voices ring out worries and distress,
Creating chaos -- escalating my stress,
So twisted and grotesque is their form,
They sound demented and so forlorn!
Their claws dig deep, leaving scars unseen,
These fiends in my mind – a lethal machine!

But the real-world fiends that roam around,
Exuding such charm and calm and sweet sound,
Yet their lingering presence and daunting might,
Are creepier than the foes that haunt my night!
Far more chilling than the ones that fill my mind -
So very scheming and devious one can never find!

Give me the fiends in my mind then,
For with them I'll make peace and be a friend,
As the ones that roam the streets are worse,
My thoughts and visions make a better universe!

(29.12.2019)

* * * * *

Break the Wall

Break the wall -
question all,
resist fear,
but be clear.
Watch a wild flower -
with little power,
blooms all day,
making its way,
with its little big might,
it puts up a good fight
casting every doubt
out!
forging on.
The sun it gazes upon -
without a helping hand
it emerges so grand
beyond the wall,

abiding by its call
pursuing its vision
finishing its mission!

(24.06.2020)

* * * *

Cancer

Using religious piety,
To spread hate in society,
Cancer masquerades, to destroy
Using every malignant ploy,
Spreading spite - feigning honesty,
Thriving well as a fallacy -
A wolf with warm deceptive eyes,
Charms one and all with its disguise.
Its rule is avid bigotry,
Feasting on the minority,
Spreading uncontrolled all-around,
All of compassion's voice is drowned.
Breaking walls; tearing hearts apart;
Hateful seeds sown in every heart.

Muzzling dissent, playing a perilous game,
Fascism is this cancer's treacherous name.

(21.03.2022)

* * * *

Canvas of Memories

On this day we often think,
Why we were taken to life's brink,
Unable to say our final goodbye,
Our souls ache, as we question why.

Though in memories we find solace and peace,
The gaps that remain will never cease.
Though we couldn't see you in action one last time,
Your being lingers on – ever so sublime!

The presence of your absence - it oft cuts deep,
Your quirky ways, into our lives does creep -
So very often, and in every place,
Our trend of thought - such memories displace!

Cherishing in our dreams where time dissolves,
Your presence, and spirit forever evolves.
And as we travel around and journey afar,
Every word unspoken becomes a shooting star!

In the canvas of memories colours blend –
A symphony of emotions without an end,
In the depths of the unknown we find true solace –
A bond unbreakable, etched in God's abiding grace.

(11.12.2022)

* * * * *

Change

The ballet of life,
many tales it conceives,
as the music plays on,
all the changes it weaves.

Spring embraces winter,
as her icy grip thaws,
and as flowers start to bloom,
nature erases the cold flaws.

Summer follows soon,
all warm sunny and bright,
painting nature's canvas,
With hues vibrant, bold and light.

Change is the motto,
as one will quickly see
autumn with prancing leaves,
dancing gleefully.

Life mirrors this rhythm
for in change lies grace,
accepting the unknown
as novel paths we trace!

(25.05.2023)

* * * * *

Chaotic Beauty

In chaos, where order goes astray,
A whirlwind of madness, surely comes to stay.
The winds of confusion, they twist and twine,
Creating a stage, where chaos does dine.

Wherein life spins in turmoil, like tops in storms,
No rhyme, rhythm or reason - just a tangle of norms.
The minds of the people, lost in utter disarray,
Caught in the tempest, where chaos holds sway.

There's no predicting, no pattern to behold,
Just a sea of disorder, where stories unfold.
The once calm waters, now turbulent and wild,
Engulfing the land in a frenzy, untamed and beguiled.

The streets are a maze, with no direction in sight,
Lost in the pandemonium, like day turning to night.
The order once known, now shattered and torn,
Replaced by the chaos, where all is forlorn!

But amidst the madness, there's a spark of light,
A glimmer of hope in the darkest of night.
For chaos brings change, where old structures fall,
Creating space for growth, for something new to install.

In the chaos, there's beauty, a chance to rebuild,
To reshape the world, with a vision fulfilled.
From the ashes of disorder, new ideas take flight,
With creativity and innovations, chaos ignites.

Let this messy beauty fuel our fire,
In its unruly presence, find what we desire.
For within the mayhem, lies a chance to explore,
To reshape the world and create something more.

So, grip the unknown and the disorder that ensues,
And realize the beauty that chaos can infuse.

(08.06.2020)

* * * * *

Compassion

In this selfish world so cold,
A beacon of light guides the way -
Its compassion's touch, a hand to hold,
And guide and brighten the day.

With gentle words and deeds of grace,
Compassion heals the wounds others bear.
It sees beyond the mask upon the face,
Showing that someone truly does care!

In empathy and kindness, one will find,
A bond that connects us heart to heart -
Lifting us up with words so kind,
Helping us to navigate life's art!

Oh, compassion is a gift so fond and true,
A gentle soothing light that sees us through!

(02.03.2019)

* * * * *

Contrary Mary

Mary, Mary quite contrary,
Your garden's a campaigner's sanctuary,
You care not for norms and codes,
Displaying authenticity as the buds unfold.
Yes, you are contrary -
As your feminist spirit is unwary,
Caring not what people say,
Striving for freedom all the way.
Seeds of empowerment you do sow.
Approving all and sundry to grow.
The royal red roses so bright,
Each petal whispering passionate might.
Determined daisies dancing in the breeze,
All norms and rules their spirit will freeze!
The tall tenacious tulips sway
In the wind, all through the day.
Bluebells, buttercups, bloom near and far,
You permit them to grow where ever they are.
So very contrary - you do not weed!
Your garden is a preserve for all indeed!

A shrubbery that's a refuge for all -
Where voices are heard, however small.
Freedom is your commitment -
Your feminist garden is a true testament!

(24.09.2022)

* * * * *

Darkness

At the beauty of the night,
I just love to stand and stare -
At the stillness and silence,
And forget all stress and care.

The darkness has great beauty,
With which nothing can compare,
No wonder God did not state –
"Let the darkness not be there".

(23.06.1993)

* * * *

Dear Angst

Within my soul a feeling does reside,
That I can never ever put aside.
The weight on my chest is heavy and deep,
A constant companion that annuls my sleep,

Oh, Angst you've consumed my very being,
And restlessness – my clear thoughts blurring.
With every breath I take, Angst's presence lingers,
Like a haunting tune sung by thousand singers.

Why do you wrap my thoughts like a twisted vine,
Tangling my mind, as though it were thine?
Worries and fears hop in my head,
With a sequence of dance steps causing dread!

In the stillness of nights where shadows loom large,
You gate crash and into my mind you barge,
Whispering doubts you gnaw at my heart,
As I sink in despair – you pretend to depart.

But as I gaze through the maze a flicker of light
I see, a silver sliver of hope shining so bright,
For Angst you unknowingly did ignite,
A fire within me to strive and to fight!

For in this struggle, resilience I have found -
Becoming stronger now I do rebound,
Realizing that in this tapestry of life, you have a place -
To remind me that in the maze strength has its space.

So, Angst though you may hover you cannot define,
My very essence and my true design!

(30.12.2019)

* * * *

Demanding Justice

Through terror ridden lands our voices roar,
With our courage untamed, our dreams we explore.
In the depths of sorrow where tears intertwine,
Our hearts are heavy with grief - yours and mine.

Ravished and raped, innocence torn apart,
Souls shattered forever, scarring the heart,
A life marked with darkness; wounds left to bear,
Molestation's vile touch, a burden so unfair.

The pain lingers on like a haunting refrain,
In the minds of every woman, causing pain
For those who endured, their anguish untold,
When monsters struck, their futures now sold.

As these fiends roam around, the rulers are blind
Or are their hearts so hardened and so unkind?
Do they not have daughters, mothers, or sisters dear,
Or does dirty politics, leave their conscience unclear?

In the lands of genocide where courage resides,
A story of strength, where hope never hides,
Midst outrageous tragedy and despair,
We rise as one demanding justice and care.

We shall not be shut down, nor live in despair,
Our spirits resilient, it is a cause we share.
In the face of adversity, we stand up tall
Demanding justice for one and all.

(20.11.2022)

* * * *

Digital Smiley

In this fleeting world, where emotions are blurred,
A symbol emerges, a smiley so absurd,
Like a band aid for cancer – a shallow disguise,
A digital smiley, devoid of true ties.
It lacks the depth of emotions within,
Just flickering on the screen - a digital grin!
A pixelated emotion just typed in,
A façade where real feelings lie thin!
So, let us not be fooled by this virtual disguise,
And engage with authenticity where true smiles arise,
By stepping into sincere reality's domain,
Where genuine echoes of the past remain!

(28.12.2023)

* * * * *

Discern

Let me learn in my own way,
Lead me not - let me stray.
Let's not kill the 'cat with curiosity'
Let me tread the path of complexity!

Instruction beyond a point is a waste,
Experiencing oneself, reveals the taste
Of knowledge and true discernment,
As this is the way to contentment!

Given formulas are but water tight,
Blurring one's vision in a beam of light.
Thinking outside the box is such a joy
So don't give me set models as a toy!

I don't think like you, you see
Knowledge needs to set me free.

(02.08.2015)

* * * *

Distress

Distress, oh how you weigh me down,
A heavy burden so hard to bear,
You grip my soul and rip my crown -
So lost as into the abyss I stare.

You come in waves, a raging storm,
A tempest so out of control.
My mind is worn, my heart is torn,
As I lie trapped in this deep dark hole.

I call out for help and for peace,
But silence alone rings in my ear,
My pain and sorrow will not cease,
As I am filled with doubt and fear.

I long for hope a ray of light -
To guide my walk through this night,
To hoist me up and help me fight,
For injustice to be set right.

Till I live I'll hold on tight,
To hope and love and what is right,
For though you may eclipse my sight,
My spirit will persist to shine bright!

(20.05.2023)

* * * * *

Does He Not Care for Me?

When God has made this great big earth,
Has planned the wonders of my birth,
Does He not then care for me?

When He has flung this earth in space,
Spinning it at a given pace,
Will He not then care for me?

When God formed the sun's golden rays,
Setting it up with its warm blaze,
Will He not then care for me?

When He has placed the moon on high,
Like a silver disc, in the night sky,
Will He not care for me?

When God has pinned each star above,
As a symbol of His abiding love,
Does He not then care for me?

When He cares for birds so small,
Numbering when each of them fall,
Will He not care for me?

When he has painted each insect's wing,
Created music for every bird to sing,
Will he not care for me?

His creation's intricate design,
Is a reflection of His love divine,
Which is a sign that He cares for me!

(14.08.2002)

* * * *

Don't Extinguish This Fire

This is a patriarchal world,
Where women have no say,
Decisions that are made
Always go the man's way.

The stage set for her
By values, codes and norms.
Makes her go through life shrouded,
Facing all her storms.

Only in his shadow,
She's made to feel secure,
But all of reality shows,
That her insecurities have no cure.

How can the perpetrators protect?
How can the predators care?
There shadow is a mere pretence,
To showcase and declare.

For senior women and girls,
Young ones and infants,
Have little public space,
Set by the world's indifference.

Yet women stand tall,
Fighting the nasty tide,
Dismantling all the chains,
Never losing their pride.

For every battle she faces,
She never cowers down,
Knowing full well that
Within her, all strength is found.

Do not silence her voice,
Her passion is not insignificant,
For she will rise up and speak out,
As her will power is magnificent!

She's a force to be reckoned with,
Don't snuff her dreams and desires,
With your rules and constraints,
You cannot extinguish such fires.

(08.03.1987)

* * * * *

Don't Judge Me

Don't judge me by my class or caste,
or creed or race,
Don't judge me by the length of my skirt,
or the beard on my face.
Don't judge me by my sexual orientation,
or gender, or lineage,
just look at me as me -
Don't try reading beyond the offered page,
just respect my identity!

Don't judge me by my riches and fame,
or the language I speak,
Don't judge me by my beliefs or my name,
and the colour on my cheek.
Don't judge me by my size or age,
the customs I follow, or my heritage,
Don't judge me by the scars that I bear,
just look at me - the simple visage
Before you - with kindness and care!

(25.08.2018)

* * * * *

Don't Lie to Me

Mirror, Mirror on the wall,
Do not lie to me at all.
For what you show me as me,
Is not true at all you see!

Don't be fooled by what you see,
The world's mirror shows not your reality,
Look beyond the reflection deep within,
And find the truth that lies therein!

(22.06.2017)

* * * *

Emptiness

Time keeps moving, life goes on,
But your absence stays, forever strong.
Five years have gone, yet the pain has remained,
A constant reminder of joy that cannot be regained.

For all the years to come, this emptiness will be,
A hollow space that only memories can see.
Though life moves forward, and moments fade away,
Your absence has come to stay, night and day.

(10.12.2024)

* * * * *

Escape

Give me a ticket
to a place and life,
that will release me,
from all bondages and cords
of artificiality,
that wraps around,
with coloured weaves
of superficiality -
created by this fake world,
that is suffocating me to death!

(03.01.2016)

* * * *

Fairy Tale?

No grand balls, no glittering gown to adorn,
Just chaos and mess in a life so forlorn.
Life is not a fairy tale or make believe,
It is but full of raw truth we must receive.

No pumpkin carriages or a midnight chime,
Just the daily duties in dust, dirt and grime,
With the mundane repetitive passing of time.

There is no prince to take you off your feet,
Struggles and fiends you will usually meet,
Life is not a fairy tale or a trendy party treat!

No magical slippers will appear - made of glass,
No magic wand will make life's problems pass,
No insightful fairy godmother will ever appear,
No way our problems and trials will disappear.

Life is not a journey so happy and neat,
Reality is complicated with challenges to meet,
So, let's teach children to stand on their feet.

The term *happily ever after* is a myth and a lie.
Do not for young ones the truth deny,
For no one, like Peter Pan from reality can fly!

(23.10.2023)

* * * *

Fall

When we tumble like a seed,
and fall
in the process break away from crazy creed.
We will fall -
but in the course shatter tradition's hold -
fall yes fall,
but rise up strong independent and bold.
After you fall,
break free from beliefs that chain – both present and past -
yes fall, but
forge ahead on a new path – firm and steadfast.
fall but rise,
and challenge foolish superstitions and crap.
Falling
is the obstacle, but it's better than the trap!
So, fall and rise
with an open mind, and a heart that's true,
for we will always fall,
while fighting for a world to be fair and new!

(08.03.2022)

* * * * *

Father – A Gift of Love

Today is Father's Day and I miss you more,
No poem or essay can express or store
The heartaches and joys I can't share,
As you are not anymore there.
I try to look for you all around,
But no one with even a semblance I've found!
Not a single relative
Who is like you – that's positive.

Unique you were and will remain
In my memory's roads and by lanes.
You were my rock, my hero, and guide
With your constant love alongside,
You taught me to be honest and kind
Never give up on truth, no matter what I find,
Stubborn you were in every way,
Always did what you would say.

Till the end you stood your ground,
A firmer person I've not yet found!
Your laughter and smile still linger on,

In my heart – this memory will never be gone.
Your cross - word and sudoku game book,
Stand as a reminder for the interest you took,
In finding solace in these games each day -
A moment of peace midst the chaos
Of sickness, and death, and painful loss-
In these small pleasures of life,
You had a getaway from the strife.

Prayerful you were in your own silent way,
As your deeds stood out as a bouquet
Of care from your garden of love,
Inspired by your faith in God's abiding love,
You lived your life with simple grace,
How can I forget the smile on your face?

On this Father's Day I thank God above'
For sending me my father - a precious gift of love

(Written for Father's Day)

(20.06.2021)

* * * * *

Fleeting

Seasons change,
and we rearrange
our lives, passing by
like the howling winds that cry.
Today we are,
but tomorrow by far -
we are not the same,
as we find ourselves in another frame!

The grass withers,
the flowers fade,
the road bends,
and life ends.
On this transient earth -
is life worth?

(03.02.2003)

* * * *

Free

A free mind and spirit
can never be
incarcerated.

Imagination soars like an eagle,
while knowledge is a cock,
that struts around - ever so feeble!

(10.11.2005)

* * * * *

Friends

What is life if we have no friend?
If we have never learned to lend?
What is life when we do not share,
Nor have a friend for whom we care?

How can we row this boat of life,
In this troubled world full of strife,
When we have never made a friend
On whom we can surely depend?

For a friend is one who would bear,
All our failures, problems, and care.
Ready even to sacrifice for you,
Supporting you, your whole life through.

And how you've spent your life depends,
On the making of such loving friends!

(05.06.1987)

* * * * *

God Cares

God's care is like a gentle breeze,
That whispers softly through the trees,
It's in the sun, the rain, the snow
In every moment, both high or low.

He watches over every bird,
That soars above - each one is heard.
He sees the smallest of seeds,
Just as he does our littlest deeds.

His care is constant, never-ending
A love so pure, it's so binding.
Through every storm and every trial,
God's care remains, faithful and loyal.

So, when you're feeling lost or small,
Remember, God sees it all.
He stands beside both night and day,
With His staff He guides the way.

And at the end, when we reach the gate
God's care awaits, complete and great.
For in His arms, we'll find sweet rest
Forevermore, among the best.

(15.09.1988)

* * * *

God's Creation

When I look at the stars above,
And hear the soft coos of the dove,
The wonder works of Thy hand,
And the golden coloured sand.

The birds I hear at the break of day,
The grass that grows along the way,
The trees that sway in the breeze,
And water that in winters freeze.

The beauty of the green blue sea,
The air we breathe so fresh and free,
The high mountains and valleys green,
With the sky above sets a perfect scene.

The sun so bright and warm does glow,
On all creatures on earth below.
The peaceful darkness of the night,
Set with the silvery moon so bright.

The lightning and thunder showers,
The thorny bushes and little flowers,
The roses and lilies white,
The violets and marigolds bright.

The sandalwood and eucalyptus trees,
Spreading their fragrance in the breeze.
Where from Lord, did you Your ideas get
To make such a lovely picture set?

(19.01.1991)

* * * *

God's Love

In the green around, and the sky so blue
One can see God's love in full view.
The unseen breeze that gently blows,
The fragrance from every rose.

We see God's love in the branches high,
In the huge trees that rise to the sky,
The rustling leaves on them sway,
As God His concerto does play!

From every birdie's sweet song,
We feel God's love all year long.
From insects, and the wasps, and bees,
From bugs and beetles, God oversees.

In the seas so vast and mountains tall,
We see God's reign o'er us all.
The waves that crash into the land,
Shows us His love ever so grand!

From vibrant reds to soothing blues,
The symphony of shades in varying hues!
The dancing colours, we see it glow,
As God's paintings, we get to know.

The beauty of the sunrise and sunset,
Shows us how each day, life is reset!
A new day, a new start -
Does boundless possibility impart.

Let us stop and take a look,
At God's amazing picture book,
For every creature, as I see,
Shows His love, that sets me free.

(24.11.1989)

* * * * *

God's Tapestry

God's hands have made the mountains high,
Daily painting the sunset sky
With gentle brushstrokes soft and low-
His tranquil beauty starts to show.

In every season His touch is felt,
In the autumn leaves as colours melt.
The flowers that dance in the breeze,
A symphony of God's harmonies.

Birds painted with the rainbow's hue
Sing songs so sweetly, tunes so true.
All around their sweet melodies flow,
This creation - a pulsating show!

The tiny sand grains on the sea shore,
Dazzling His glory for evermore.
The vast galaxies in cosmic flight,
The specks of stardust shining so bright.

And as God's hand the embroidery does weave,
With every stitch His love does interleave.
A sonnet of creation, so profound,
In every detail His kind grace is found.

God is the author of eternity.
Set in perfect time - in His tapestry.

(04.08.1994)

* * * *

Greed

In this world of poverty and strife,
Let us, let go of this selfish life.
True fulfilment lies in not what we possess,
But in the love and empathy we can express.

We chase after money and gold so bright,
Blinded by greed's deceptive light.
What do we gain by holding it all,
When others around in poverty fall?

For when we give up on our greed,
We'll form a new world where all succeed.
Stack and store not, give away with grace,
Creating a world where each have their space.

Break free from greed's binding chain,
Then kindness and generosity will reign.
This should be our creed to guide all we do,
Sharing and giving is what we must pursue!

(03.01.1989)

* * * * *

Grow Unaffected

Born but in dirty stagnant waters,
The lotus flower attains full beauty,
All protected pure and pristine,
It reaches perfect hue and majesty.

Beautiful bold and brilliant in visage,
The rose too grows all bright and sweet,
With a pure tender perfection,
Amidst the nasty thorns at its feet.

So too, in this nefarious world,
We must grow to our perfect beauty,
Unaffected by this world of strife,
Just pure in heart and honest in duty.

(04.01.1981)

* * * * *

Hope in the Rope

Deep in a heart, where shadows reside,
A soul lies wasted, with no place to hide.
Anxiety - a burden weighing on the heart -
Pushing, pulling, peeling, and tearing apart.

The soul within, with gloom hovering overhead,
As a dark veil of despair – a mind full of dread,
With no sight of nerve – not even a shred,
No light to brighten the path, left to tread.

As depression whispers - not enough
You need to be made of tougher stuff!
The soul crumbles within with no hope
But from the ceiling, where hangs the rope.

In this chaos, strength could have been found,
If only friends and family had turned things around!

(29.06.2023)

* * * * *

Hypocrisy

Words so sweet on their tongue,
But actions evil, foul and wrong,
Preaching compassion and grace -
Wearing a mask upon their face.

In shadows they lurk, their true selves concealed,
Their warped motives, never fully revealed,
Manipulating truths to fit their narrative,
Their deceitful ways - so repulsive and abrasive.

Their deeds betray their spoken creed,
A façade of lies of this fallen breed,
Their double standards are plain to see,
Reveals their lives of hypocrisy!

(25.06.2021)

* * * * *

India

A quaint land of vibrant hues, India's charm is ever true!
From majestic mountains, with scenic sunsets, sunrises to
view.
The striking nature, birds and beasts are treasures to behold.
Gorgeous beaches, and skies painted in red, pink, and gold!
The dense forests are a home to a vibrant community,
Who protect the sacred groves and live in quiet harmony.
Rivers like the life lines flowing through the land,
The waterfalls like ornaments, that are so very grand.

But from the bustling cities and quiet village lanes,
Cries of victims rise - stifled or ignored as unheard refrains!
Rape and molestations – a cruel reality,
Haunting the streets, stripping the weak of all dignity.
Women and girls face lurking demons of the night,
Preying on the vulnerable, extinguishing their light.
All ye spectators – why do you silent remain?
Does the plight of the voiceless not cause you pain?
A nation's shame, a crime that scars and sears,
Haunting echoes that will repeat every day of all the years!

In this realm of stony silence, a deafening sound we hear -
Of apathy and callousness that fills us with utter fear!
In this dominion of pitiless quiet, there is a thunderous sound
Of complete coldness where only indifference is found!
The voiceless are forgotten their pain cast aside,
No one cares for them - who have constantly cried.
While those who protest – their voices are suppressed,
Prejudice reigns supreme as folks are oppressed.

Yet we will not surrender - India arise, and guide our way,
To build a robust future where all can safely stay.
Oh, India let us cast aside the shadows that loom,
With harmony and respect - let our future beautifully bloom.

(22.12.2012)

* * * * *

In Every Falling Tear

In the garden of my heart a flower blooms,
A memory of you dear mother – so true,
Each petal, reminds me of your love - that looms
Still around me, like the morning dew.

A year has gone by yet your spirit does remain,
A guiding light in the shadows of my days.
In moments of joy, success, and pain
Your love surrounds me in countless ways.

Memories of your laughter, your gentle touch –
Echo softly in the chambers of my soul,
I long to hear your voice, I miss you so much
In this world without you, I feel less than whole.

I miss your prayers, songs and loving embrace,
Your insight and wit, your kind and gentle ways.
In my heart you hold a special hallowed space.
A love unbroken that nothing can ever erase!

In the stillness of the night, I feel your absence keen,
Three sixty-five days and your presence lingers still
Dearest mother you will in my heart be ever seen,
Your impact on me – a void no time can ever fill!

Though you're not around, your love lingers here,
In every whispered prayer and in every falling tear.

(18.02.2024)

* * * *

In God's Time

All our times are in God's hand,
And though we do not understand
Or life's commas, and full stops –
Our success and our awful flops,
We know that our God doth reign,
Change His plan – we'll strive in vain!
For in His care our days are secure,
His guidance is steadfast and sure.

God keeps the times and seasons,
If we have faith, we don't need reasons,
Only trusting in His loving care –
For the path ahead He doth prepare.
In His wisdom He guides us through
Every challenge, every breakthrough.

He knows each plan He has for us,
Filled with love, care and purpose.
Let us then trust His divine will,

Surrendering to His perfect skill.
Finding refuge in His sovereignty,
During times of intense insecurity.

Trusting God to steer our journey's course,
With His love as our guiding force,
For God in His mercy will navigate –
His timing is never ever late,
For He is the author of eternity's story,
And under His wings we find peace and glory.

(02.08.1993)

* * * * *

Invisible Hands

Adam Smith, in economic theory did proclaim -
That the unseen hand guided the markets' flame.
But concealed in the shadows lies a truth one must unveil,
The invisible hands of women – their work never does fail.

At home they toil, cooking, collecting, cleaning, caring.
Their labour undervalued in the market ever so glaring.
Is it not their invisible hands that so labour unseen -
That drives the market and the economy's machine?

Oh, Mr. Smith do you see the irony so clear,
The driving force is not what seems to appear,
For capitalism's essence is to exploit – stark and severe!

The invisible hands of women for ever strong and true,
Without their contribution what will capitalism do?

(15.11.2015)

* * * * *

I See Thy Hand

In the endless blue sky,
With numerous stars on high,
The noon day sun so bright,
And the silvery moon at night,
I see Thy hand.

In the tiny wild flowers,
That bloom for few hours,
In the different shades of green,
That sets a perfect scene,
I see Thy hand.

In the birds that always sing,
And in every little thing,
In the tiny grains of sand,
And in the mountains so grand,
I see Thy hand.

In the rose and the thorn,
In the twilight and the dawn,
In sunshine and the rain,
In happiness and in pain

I see Thy hand.

In the cool refreshing breeze,
And the rustling of the trees,
In the joyful laughter of a child –
And in moments calm and mild,
I see Thy hand.

In the echoes of a distant call,
In memories I oft recall,
In the dance of shadows in the light,
And the quiet of the deep dark night,
I see Thy hand.

In the sound of nature's song,
In moments that do not last long,
In the beauty all around,
In the silence and the sound,
I see Thy hand.

In the blend of joy and strife,
In the ebb and flow of my life,
I see Thy hand guiding me through,
In all I am and all I do!

(18.04.1986)

* * * * *

I Sit and Think

I sit and think about the beauty of the world,
Where nature's wonders are daily unfurled,
The trees that sway in the gentle breeze,
The flowers that bloom with so much ease.

The birds that sing their sweet refrain,
A melody that soothes all my pain,
The sun that rises and sets in the sky,
Painting the canvas with hues that never die.

The rivers that flow with gentle grace,
Carving out a path through time and space,
The mountains that stand so tall and proud -
Making a glorious statement ever so loud.

I sit and think of the beauty of it all,
Natures symphony so large and small,
In every vein of every leaf -
I can see God's gift of eternity!

(02.01.1999)

* * * * *

Lament of a Tree

All weak, alone and depressed I stand,
No one will ever understand
What through life, I have had to face,
As the world ate up all the space,
It always had for me!
And now you can all see,
How I am lifeless and shut down,
Due to the greedy seeds sown,
Of development and growth,
Ravishing the planet earth
Polluting the air
Oh, what despair!
Just to live in glamour and style
Reducing me to a garbage pile!

(15.10.2020)

* * * * *

Let Me Be

You dictate to me
Telling me how to be,
you strap me down,
and then you frown
if I break free,
to be who I want to be!

Yes, I do not fit
I won't stand or sit,
as you try to school,
dominate and rule
defining me to be!
what you desire to see.

How can you desire,
to light a specific fire
quelling other flames within me?
Oh, what expectation
and determination
to snuff out the me in me!

Deciding for me
to be or not to be!
how can you ever
make me want, what you prefer?

(23.08.2011)

* * * *

Life

Life comes in shades of grey,
Nothing is static or here to stay.
Don't look for just black and white,
Nothing is cut or dry or in plain sight.

In the tapestry of life, threads intertwine
Creating mysteries - unique and divine,
Accept your stories, let them slowly unfold,
Don't separate the threads –bleak, bright or bold!

(05.03.2018)

* * * *

Lilo Dearest Lilo

_(07.05.2012 – 19.10.2022)_

In the vast tapestry of life, we weave -
There are friends like you – so hard to conceive.
In this transient world your friendships', so rare -
A dear friend like you is beyond compare!
In this fleeting world – a shining star,
Dear four-legged friend, where ever you are -
I think of the years you brought such glee,
A delightful mate so happy and carefree.

Lilo dear, with starry eyes so bright,
Your curly tail, was a true delight!
I miss you so, my dear little friend,
Your presence gone - I can't comprehend
How for so many years you brought such joy,
A loyal companion, our heart's warm envoy.
Though you are no longer by my side,
In my heart your pawprints reside.

Your plate, towel, and chair, left behind
Bittersweet reminders in my mind.
Lilo, we named you after that cartoon tale
Of *Lilo and Stitch* – your memory will prevail!
The terrace was your sanctuary, your retreat,
Amongst the potted plants, you found solace sweet -
Chasing wasps, bees, and crows with glee,
You barked, and pranced about so very free.

I believe you're in heaven, in the realms above,
Surrounded by bliss and eternal love,
Sure, you are reveling in the heavenly space,
A good soul like you will find peace and grace.
So, rest in peace up there on high,
Watching the angels flying by!
Lilo my friend I miss you so,
Our bond will surely continue to grow!

(Written for our little pug - Lilo)

(19.10.2023)

* * * * *

Little Things

The mist clears,
and I do see,
the warm bright day
that dawns on me.
The bud opens,
to a pretty flower,
imparting fragrance
hour by hour.

All through the day
the little bird sings,
her sweet music
what joy it brings!

The silent moon
peeps at night,
and I do see
its silvery light.

The sky is spotted
with little stars bright,

twinkling constantly
the darkness they fight.

As the night wanes out,
the dawn is on its way,
with a gentle breeze
Welcoming a new day.

(19.04.1987)

* * * *

Live for Today

We are anxious about tomorrow,
Missing out on the joys of today,
Worrying about numerous problems,
That may never cross our way.

God takes care of all our tomorrows,
Cares of today is but yours and mine,
Bank on God who is ever faithful,
Let us just live one day at a time.

If God clothes lilies, so fair and bright,
And cares for the sparrows in their flight.
Much more will He care for you and me,
For we are precious as per His decree,

(03.04.1993)

* * * * *

Look for God

When life seems without a ray,
And you often cease to pray.
When the cross is too heavy
And you are faint and weary –
Look for Him, He's by your side.
When everything seems to fail,
And the ship does not sail,
When the shore is out of sight,
And the waves are hard to fight –
Look for Him, amidst the tide.
Through the desert sands,
Blinded alleys and barren lands,
When the mountain is too high,
And the valley, but echoes your cry,
Look for Him – your only Guide.
When the path ahead is long,
And you're tired and forlorn,
When the course you cannot trace,
And all you need is God's grace
Look for Him, He's close beside.

When your life's in confusion,
Your plans – a mere illusion.
When all friends have forsaken,
And you have been mistaken,
Look for Him, in you He abides!

(06.05.1993)

* * * * *

Lost

When one is abolished,
from memory and
erased from history –
When the truth one speaks,
is turned into a
comprehensive lie...
When one becomes
a nonentity,
and
has no identity.
When
the repeated untruths,
are believed to be the truth,
and
one has been turned into a monster,
in people's minds.

It is then and only then,
one has truly lost!

(30.05.2016)

* * * * *

Love

When the roaring waves,
Embraced the land,
When the sunbeams kissed the sand,
They held their hands,
Gazing at the sea -
Their love setting them free.

As the moon rose up high,
In the dark night sky,
Casting shadows gentle and light,
They whispered well into the night -
Their love shining ever so bright,
Finding perfect solace and delight.

In the stillness of the night,
'Neath the starry sky so bright,
Their loving thoughts danced,
Their endearing feelings pranced,
Setting their caring hearts aglow
In love, that only they could know!

(10.02.2020)

* * * * *

Maternal Memories

Memories bring back your loving face,
A presence that time cannot erase,
I miss you with each passing year,
The absence of your presence is etched so clear!

Your face a beacon in my mind,
Our spirits yet remain intertwined,
The essence of your life lingers near,
In this space and time, I hold so dear.

Each day I feel the echo of your grace,
But on this your birthday I do confess,
The ache of your absence fills every space
As I miss your laughter, music and sweet embrace.

In my memories your love and prayers always stay,
Guiding me onwards, every step of the way.
Though you are gone your love will always stay,
Those cherished memories will guide my way.

(02.03.2024)

* * * * *

Me, Myself and I

I find solace in solitude deep,
A space so sacred I love to keep
It to myself, for me and I -
A place where there can be no lie.
Away from the deafening din,
I have the moments with myself to pin
My thoughts, then deliberately unfold
Playing with emotions yet untold,
Away from all the loud chatter,
The silence that is defied by clatter,
Is found by my isolation,
A comfort filled consolation,
To discover the depths of my soul,
Which thereby makes me complete and whole.

There is no guise, façade, or mask,
Just an innocuous zone to bask,
Confronting all my deepest fears,
And washing them off with copious tears.
With introspection I find release,

In this calm I find accord and peace.
Talking with me, myself, and I -
Slowly life's sense will amplify,
Setting a complete paradigm,
In a ringing melodic rhyme.

(06.06.2020)

* * * * *

My Abstract Reality

In this crowded noisy room,
I close my eyes and take a flight
Into the rooms of my mind,
And the comfort of its night.

Into my world of abstract thought,
Where imagination can't be bought,
I see the colours all around,
Shapes forming from the ground.
And stepping into this reality,
I see a whole new imagery -
Lines blurring the known from the unknown,
And what is beyond my senses is shown -
A symphony of incredible ingenuity,
A melody of awesome creativity,
In the sanctuary of my mind
Where dreams are intertwined,
Where secrets are safe to keep,
And my emotions run so deep.
A place where I can explore,

As I enter through the allegorical door.
In this place I can truly be -
An echo of my abstract reality,
I merge in with total harmony -
A vast space of endless possibility,
Where imagination becomes a reality.

Needless is the crowded room,
For all noise is snuffed out,
I am at peace in my abstraction
Of this reality – there's no doubt!

(09.05.2021)

* * * *

My Daughter

You my daughter, a friend for life,
A pillar of constant strength,
Midst the maddening strife,
You stand by to any length!
In your heart compassion flows so pure,
Your loving support is there for sure.
Through every trial you remain strong and true,
My daughter, my friend I thank God for you!
In your smile I find endless grace,
The bond we have time can never erase.
In your laughter I find solace and delight,
Your presence a beacon in the darkest night.
With every step you take a rich legacy you sow,
A bond unbreakable that will forever grow,
Hats off to you my only daughter so dear,
A source of joy and love – year after year!
Your spirit shines bright – a guiding light,
A friend for life, through every plight.
You are sparkling and rare,
A precious priceless gem -

A treasure beyond compare.
And from you will always stem,
Brutally honest emotions and care,
That will shine brightly I know,
Here or there or anywhere,
Like the sunbeams that always glow!

(20.04.2022)

* * * * *

My Father - A Gem so Rare

God gave me a father a gem so rare,
Whose love was untainted – beyond compare.
He lived his life with a heart so pure,
With values rooted in Christ, steadfast and secure.

He taught me lessons, both big and small,
To work hard and give it my all.
His words were few, but his actions spoke,
And in our loving God he found true hope.

Steady and persistent in every way,
He constantly did what he would say,
Till the end he stood his ground,
A firmer person I've not yet found!

Prayerful he was in a quiet way,
His deeds stood out as a fond bouquet!
My father a person, so full of grace,
His love and kindness, was a warm embrace.

None on earth can replace the void he left,
But in my heart, his spirit I have kept.
I cherish the fun and mirth we did share,
Memories that will always linger out there!

On every one of his birthdays I do reflect,
On the love and wisdom, he did project.
Though tears do fall, and my heart does ache,
I thank God above, for the legacy he did make.

He lived his life with simple grace,
How can I forget the smile on his face?
I thank you every day Holy Father above,
For sending me my father - a precious gift of love!

(07.10.2023)

* * * * *

My Identity

My true identity,
lies in the depth of me,
where I am lost,
in the shades of my mind.
So very elusive
and hard to find
me in the maze
of my soul's design,
as myself in me
are so intertwined!
I search the key,
to unlock the truth
and set myself free -
but drowned am I in me.
Hence, I can never know myself
or my true Identity!

(24.09.2017)

* * * * *

Monsters

In the depths of my mind, monsters reside,
Their size growing with each stride,
In layers of my thought, they hide.

Whispering doubts, and casting shadows long,
These monsters with teeth real strong,
The darkness they so prolong!

Real monsters parading I oft believe,
Their sweet talks so well deceive -
Truth from lie one can't perceive!

I will run, and I will hide,
I will not let them inside,
Nor permit them to stand beside.

Learn their tricks and beat their game,
They can't cloud my anxious frame,
In this clash of the mind, success I'll claim.

From these monsters I shall flee,
For then in peace, I shall be!
Adrift on the sea of serenity.

(08.09.2020)

* * * * *

Nature's Murmur

Chirping songs so sweet and clear,
Bringing cheer to all who hear,
Very early in the morn,
Even before the day is born.

She starts her merry little song,
That rings out clear all day long,
Snowy winters or rainy days,
She will sing her song of praise.

Her sweet song banishes strife,
As branches bare, come to life.
Her bright eyes and tiny beak
Symbolising all that is meek.

She flies around so very fast -
Her wings a whisper in the vast!
She flits and darts full of grace,
My cell phone's lens can't keep pace
To capture her cute form and face.

Nature's murmur, so tough to trace! –
From dawn to dusk there's no rest,
Oh, tiny bird full of zest -
I wonder what is your quest?
Little red breast you bring joy near,
Tiny Robin, I hold you dear.

(01.05.2023)

* * * * *

No Dynamic Drama

In the darkness, beauty works.
Watch the plants grow,
as from seeds they
sprout.

Nature nurtures noiselessly,
no dynamic drama on the dais,
persisting purposefully without a
doubt!

Is it not then true
that work can be
done in silence too,
or when the lights are
out?

There is no need for drama,
or a fog horn kind of
shout!

(02.11.2012)

* * * * *

Ode to Darkness

You make the stars shine,
And give us hope every time,
Oft condemned as evil -
And made to represent the devil.

Anyone who walks through your gate,
Is warned of meeting a fearful fatal fate -
For in the shadows so deep, you dwell
So misunderstood with a curious tale to tell!

Little do we realize,
That when you materialize,
You underline the presence of light -
And all that is shining and bright!

Your beauty is beyond compare,
And the courageous who ever dare
To tread through you, will find a gleam -
A hopeful twinkle – a sparkling dream!

(04.12.2015)

* * * * *

Ode to the Pencil

In a world of words and lines so fine,
The pencil's life begins to shine-
A slender shaft of graphite and wood,
It works to create all that is good.
From sketches bold to notes so neat,
As it waltzes on a blank sheet -
Creating designs and stories of our days,
Writing a poem, a prose, a phrase.
Sharpened oft it is poised to create,
An artist's vision that often does captivate,
In the hands of a dreamer both young and old –
As their stories are scripted – memories unfold!

Hats off to the pencil – so simple and profound,
With a leaden heart – yet so much grace is found!

(07.05.2013)

* * * * *

Ode to the Women of the Earth

Through the valleys, and hills our voices roar,
With our courage untamed, our dreams we explore -
In the depths of sorrow, where tears intertwine,
Our hearts are heavy with grief - yours and mine.
Ravished and raped, innocence torn apart,
Souls shattered forever, scarring the heart,
A life marked with darkness; scars left to bear -
Molestation's vile touch, a burden so unfair.
In darkness they stand, as their stories unfold,
Monsters' wrath unleashed; their destinies sold.
The agony lingers on like a haunting refrain
In the minds of every woman, causing pain
In this their plight, their bodies bear scars
As politics scripts the battle ground of wars!
These fiends roam around, the rulers are blind
Or are their hearts so hardened and so unkind?
Women dear Women your story we'll tell,
All know your daunting spirits won't quell.

(27.07.2023)

* * * * *

Our Callous World

Folks as usual passed her by,
each of them had their work.
few paused to look,
some stopped to sigh,
others tossed a coin,
and hurried by.
All forsook
she lay, crumpled and dirty,
gaunt, and weak, and sick.
not spoken to –
not cared for –
not loved –
who could spare the time,
in this non-stop world
to wait upon her?
So, there she lay
day after day
watching people pass her by.
Life of the beggar
was sure so forlorn,

and as years pass by
she would soon be gone,
no one could care less
to even remember!
All we do is exploit the poor,
by earning credit
framing policies
to alleviate poverty!
All our actions are but paradoxical,
and life's a sham, and so hypocritical!

(03.08.1986)

* * * * *

Our Life – A Farce

Selfishness and ruthless greed,
have enslaved all of us indeed,
when we choose to kill,
to accomplish our will,
to cheat and embellish,
plagiarize ideas and publish
without any trace of guilt,
our little 'empires' are built,
with bribery, nepotism and jingoism,
on the foundation of communalism,
cemented by religious fundamentalism,
adorned by casteism, sexism and racism,
all in the garb of secularism!
Our life is nothing but a sham,
we tout our virtues, but it is all a scam!

Are we civilized since ages past,
is not our way of life a tragic farce?

(05.09.1990)

* * * * *

Peace of Mind

Bring in peace,
and joy release.
build bridges,
not walls.
mend fences,
heed calls.
loosen the chain,
abort all pain,
love and embrace,
with abiding grace.
Let our passion
be compassion.
Then we'll find,
peace of mind!

(17.08.2016)

* * * * *

Scars

She sat by the rubble of her broken home,
her tear-filled eyes stared at the torn rag doll –
The doll she had made with rags for her doll,
whose head was smashed by the falling missiles.
or was it a brick that was used by the ones,
who worship in another way, eat different food,
or dress differently and love a different colour?
Did differences do this to my smashed doll,
And to the doll's doll?
She looked for a pen below the
broken glass – searched for paper but
found none.
Using the broken glass – she etched the word
'Different dolls'
on her skin –
She felt no pain – as greater pain lay before her.
New scars – yes, to remember the old ones,
scars that cannot be forgotten,

and shouldn't be by the mute spectators,
scars that should never have been etched
on skin, or in the memories of the innocent.

(26.04.2022)

* * * * *

Sadness

Sadness is a cloak I wear,
to hide the tears, I cannot shed;
A mask I wear to face the glare,
of life and all the things, I dread.

Sadness is a silent voice,
that speaks to me of things unknown;
A whisper in the night that cloys
my soul with thoughts of things undone.

Sadness is a dream of things,
that never were, nor ever shall;
A longing for the unattainable,
that makes my heart with sorrow fall.

Sadness is a part of me,
that I must bear until I die;
A shadow on my life's clear sea,
a cloud that dismisses the sunlit sky.

But yet I love my sadness too,
for it has taught me many things;
It has made me strong, showing me through
the tragic trails that lead to spring.

And so, I wear my cloak of sadness
with pride, and face the world unafraid;
For I have learnt that sadness is
the touchstone of the soul's true blade.

(19.01.2020)

* * * *

Seen Them?

Seen the little flowers
that bloom along the way?
Heard the little birds
that sing all day?

Felt the green grass
soft 'neath your feet?
Seen the setting of leaves
on branches, so neat?

Seen the little bee
visiting flower from flower?
Never getting tired
working hour by hour!

Seen a buffalo?
Look into her eyes,
its depth you'll never know,
nor what thought in them lies!

Try and trace the bird,
when from a tree it sings,
seen the different colours
painted on its wings?

Seen the tall palms,
swaying in the breeze?
Counted the branches
on the different trees?

Seen the little plants,
that grow on a hillside?
Though on a steep slope
by faith they do abide!

Though unnoticed
are such details, by all
God sure is meticulous
in all things great and small.

(18.04.1986)

* * * *

Silent Echoes

The sound of silence rings out clear,
A deafening echo one can clearly hear.
As the world once vibrant, now stands still
In the grip of Covid's unspoken chill.
Isolation drapes me with a heavy shroud,
The ricochet of quiet – like a deadly cloud.
The touch of a loved one - a memory dear,
Now replaced by sadness, gloom and fear.
In solitude I find myself confined,
With a chaotic symphony in my mind,
Days and nights blurred out in time,
Wondering what could be my crime?
The laughter of children – a distant dream,
Like the fading of mist on a soundless stream.

Life's rhythm is now so out of time,
A lurid long loud melancholic chime,
Missed beats and rests in this melody,

Or is it a jarring heartbroken symphony,
Played by the mesmerized moon,
Observing this world of gloom?

(04.05.2020)

* * * * *

Simplicity

With disorder cleared, minds at ease,
A simple life will render peace,
No great drives and grand desires,
Just the joy of 'now' one acquires.

A cup of tea, a book in hand,
The small pleasures we understand,
A simple flower, a gentle breeze,
The petals waving with mild ease,
A sunset's glow, a starry night,
The deep darkness studded with light.

No need for excess or for show,
Or pretend more than one does know.
Simplicity is not to lack,
It is to declutter and unpack.
To focus on what matters most,
Resting as Simplicity's host.

Breaking free from this muddled mess,
One finds peace, joy and grand success!

(25.03.2019)

* * * * *

Sister of Mine

We've shared our joys, tears, and fights.
Discussed issues of wrongs and rights.
From baby memories to adult years,
Our bond as sisters has lulled our tears.

We've argued about toys, clothes, time, and space,
But in the end our love has found its place.
Through life's ups and downs our thoughts don't align,
Yet in our differences, a paradoxical bond we design.

In divergent paths we find a common ground,
In our uniqueness we blend a harmonious sound.
I'm grateful for our subtle jokes and fun that brings a grin,
For memories we've made and the ones we are still in.

In our little gardens we've shared a love so green,
In gardening and exchanging plants our bond is seen.
We've planted seeds and watched them grow,
Nurturing life, as sisters, a tie that will always show.

You're more than a sister, you're a friend and guide,
Not a partner-in-crime, yet our love will never subside.
Through life's adventures we've travelled far and wide,
Alone at times, but sometimes side by side.

From mountains high, and oceans so blue,
Our experiences always shining through,
But more than any place or memory we hold,
It's our shared faith in Christ, that makes us bold.

Our parents taught us about His love so true,
In Sunday school, church, songs sung and all we'd do.
Our continuing faith in Jesus allays every fear,
As the vicissitudes of life, we continue to steer.

Yet our interests diverge like the branches on a tree,
You're hooked on to crochet, creating beauty to see.
I am into art as painting is my passion,
But both are far from fads and fashion!

My interest was in sports and races on the field,
Yours was in dance, with rhythms that joys yield.
You can whip up a storm, with spices in a flair,
I'll take a seat and enjoy the meal you gladly share.

You're gentle and kind – a soul serene and free,
While I'm outspoken – a spirit wild and free.
You walk by faith with a heart full of trust and might,
My mind is full of doubt and "what-ifs" through the night!

Our academic interests were so different you see,
You're so crazy about Physics, unraveling mystery.
The laws of motion and the cosmos' might,
Fascinates your mind and ignites your light.

I, on the other hand, delve into Economics' sway,
Understanding the markets and the global way.
The subject enthralls me – a complex web to unwind,
Grasping markets, trade, currencies – a puzzle so intertwined.

Sister of mine, our love and loyalty will forever remain -
This treasure and friendship our life will always sustain.

*(Written for my one and only sister –
Dr. Beulah J.M. Rajkumar)*

(18.01.2025)

* * * * *

Smile

Smile along the way,
All through the day,
Then a lonely soul may find,
Happiness and peace of mind.

Smile along the way,
And let your smile stay,
Then a grieving soul who has cried,
Will have all her tears dried.

Smile along the way,
It could be your friend's mainstay,
And she could combat all her grief,
Confidently finding some relief.

Smile along the way,
All through the day,
Then a wounded broken heart.
Would be aided for a new start.

(15.05.1981)

* * * * *

Sorrow

My grief consumes me -
Though I try to break free,
The weight is too heavy,
The light I cannot see -
My eyes are filled with tears,
Dripping down my face, like rain
On my dirty window pane.

No hope - no dreams,
All flown down the streams.
Gnawing me is my sorrow
As I think about the morrow.

Depended on the happy forever,
But realised this is a big lie -
As everyone is left alone,
With memories that make one cry!

The hollowness is unbearable,
The path ahead is irreplaceable -

As that's the only route laid out,
That one must tread, without a doubt.

(07.05.2020)

* * * * *

Surrealism

Eerie shadows dance in the moon's light,
A world of wonder – both dark and bright,
The strangeness of the deep dark night -
Sends down a shiver – a curious fright.

Imagination weaves a fabric of dreams,
Where reality and illusion flow as streams,
In this furtive world where truth is blurred -
Our deepest dread and qualms are stirred!

In this shadowy world we see our fears,
Where fantasy dressed up oft appears -
A quirky tapestry, a mosaic so bizarre -
In this surrealism we see who we are!

(17.12.2019)

* * * * *

Thanks!

Thank you, Lord,
for another day,
and all the blessings
You send my way,
with a grateful heart,
I earnestly pray.

Though storms may arise,
and my boat is rocked,
my hope never dies,
and my faith is not mocked.

In Your perfect peace,
and Your kind embrace,
all doubts and fears cease,
with Your tender grace.

Your strength is enough,
in challenging times,
Your love engulfs me,
as I scale each climb.

I'll sail fearlessly,
With You by my side,
Your mercy endures,
through every high tide.

Thank you Lord,
for another night,
and all the comfort,
You always provide,
through darkest hours,
Your love will never subside!

(22.09.1993)

* * * *

The Bridge

In my dreamy sky a bridge appears,
A structure made of celestial thread -
Connecting the present, and past years,
Where my dreams and reality wed.

Stepping on the bridge, the unknown I face,
As boundaries blur, and time begins to bend,
I journey to the realm of outer space,
Where wonders will seemingly never end.

Dear bridge of dreams a portal to my soul,
Where wild imagination takes control.
I walk upon this bridge forever changed,
In the land of dreams, I am rearranged.

Now on this bridge I stand and contemplate,
As it holds a pensive way to recreate.

(23.08.2021)

* * * * *

The Crevice

Near an unkempt wall it grew,
Elegant beautiful, and bright.
Watered by the morning dew,
It shone with charming light.

And as it grew fair and tall,
To a greater and ample height,
It chanced upon a crevice in the wall
Where in, it met a ray of light.

Guided by this beam so bright,
The creeper grew with increased strength,
No one could see it push and fight,
As it quietly snuck the crevices' length.

Creeping through the crack to the other side,
Broadening its visual point of view.
With no apprehension nor pride,
To a tall flowering beauty, it grew.

Crevices often cause us to grieve,
Making our past failures to recall.
Worry not but hope receive,
For the sun shines beyond the wall!

(19.11.2020)

* * * * *

The Flower Arrangement

Looking at leaves and flowers so bright,
The arrangements in vases - a wondrous sight,
Each bloom chosen, with love and care,
To Display the beauty God crafted so rare!

The arrangement drives out every gloom,
As it takes center stage lighting up the room.
Speaking of beauty and nature's design,
A fragrant sonnet so quiet and sublime!

Roses so bold, the lilies standing tall,
Carnations add charm, the peonies enthrall.
Set together in a vase – a floral display -
I bask in the joy the flowers convey.

In each arrangement there's a story untold -
As the flowers in display slowly unfold.

(02.05.2024)

* * * * *

The Full Stop

A small dot, a punctuation mark,
Like a tiny little spark.
Bringing a sentence to an end,
A time to think, and a time to send
Added ideas to my mind,
Fresh views and perspectives to find.
May be a place to pause for some rest,
To weave the ideas with new zest.
In music and in text, rests play a part,
Helping in creating a lovely work of art,
Finding a place, oh so calm -
A time to hum a melodic psalm!
A full stop could convey a change,
Shuffle thoughts, or rearrange.
Most philosophies to start anew,
And fresh insights one can pursue!

(21.07.2023)

* * * * *

The Little Sparrow

In the hush of dawn,
The little sparrow's song -
A once familiar melody
Has faded and gone!
Our existence is tinged
With nostalgic sorrow,
As we miss the tiny
Shaded brown sparrow.
The greed of humans
Has changed the scene,
And left our vibrant world
So noisy, dusty and less serene!
But hope does linger in the air,
As nature fights
Back beyond compare,
For through all destruction
She stands grand and tall -
Defying all odds both great and small,
Emerging victorious from every fall!

For I've seen the sparrow return,
With her little wings unfurled,
On my terrace every morning,
Bringing joy to this
Wounded world.

(03.02.2024)

* * * *

The Palette

From the depths of my mind,
A world of wonder I find,
Where ideas drift free,
And creativity flows like the sea.
Through the art I create,
Voicing that which I can't articulate,
The hidden beauty emanates,
And colourful joy permeates.
On the canvas as I paint,
With vibrant views I acquaint.

In a world of fear where shadows convene,
Where hope is but a distant dream,
And the sun is rarely ever seen,
My art springs up a realm so serene -
The colours of my palette speak,
In every form and every streak,
Sketching out a story once lived,
In my mind 's eye – so vivid!

(23.08.2022)

* * * * *

The Phoenix

She dies a million times,
yet she lives
in her loneliness,
among so many folks.
As for her, the sun shines in
her cyclones.
She faces numerous trials,
yet she stands up firm!
Losing many battles,
she finally wins the war.
Weeps innumerable times
smiling through it all!
Is broken, battered betrayed,
traumatised, tormented, traded,
discarded, demonised, destroyed,
yet continues to live…
for she is beautiful
and strong,
and in her abstraction

so very real!
Yes, she is a woman
she is every woman I have met,
she is me!

(08.03.2019)

* * * *

The Prostitute

They turned her into a *keep*,
Keeping her life and her *cash*,
Cashing in on her *identity*,
Identifying her with the scum of *society*,
Socializing others to believe that she is *sin*,
Sinning against her very *being*,
Being the monster in her reality
Real relationships for her now makes no *sense*
Sensing the mess in her *life*
Living death is her present tense!

(18.10.1995)

* * * *

The Stroke

Every stroke tells a story -
A tale of joy or sorrow,
Copious passions of yesteryears,
And hopes and fears for tomorrow.

With every stroke of the brush,
Sentiments visibly unfold
In vibrant hues, and shades quite dull,
The stories of the past are told.

A single stroke, a tender shade,
Whispers secrets untold,
Of love, of loss, of dreams, and doubts,
Details of myriad stories unfold.

As the colours dance in display,
Each stroke a conduit of expression -
Captures moments words can't convey,
Translating them to graphic impressions!

(24.09.2022)

* * * * *

The Window

Oh, window a portal to the world outside,
A frame capturing moments passing by,
Through you I glimpse the world so wide,
And feel the gentle breeze's whispering sigh.

You are the stage to a majestic display,
A superb canvas, where the sun's rays dance
Between the low branches that sway,
With the soft dreamy clouds floating in a trance.

Oh, dear window you are more than just a frame,
You bear witness to silent scenes divine,
And through you I do the past reclaim,
As you capture prized moments frozen in time.

So, as I gaze through the windowpane
I recollect life's transient refrain.

*(In memory of my grandma, who used to sit and gaze out of her
window in Tambaram, Chennai)*

(24.06.1988)

* * * *

Their Mission

Against the wall
the roses stood tall –
bright and bold,
like days of old,
there was no fear,
their agenda clear –
in the corner to shine,
and never to whine,
sun or rain, wind or hail,
their mission was to prevail!

With petals soft and fragrance sweet,
their beauty a wondrous sight to greet,
a symbol of their mission clear -
blooming in the corner without any fear.
Standing against the wall with great pride,
in their vibrant colours side by side.
A testament to nature's lovely art -
etching their mission in every heart!

(28.08.2006)

* * * * *

The Unknown

There is a zone
where the sun rises
but there is no light!
Where birds fly around
with no fluttering sound.
Where flowers and trees
stand withered.
Where stars shine
yet there is no glimmer.
The ocean waves rise and fall
beneath the shining moon
Ever so silently!
All this is
seen but never noticed,
touched but never felt
heard yet never listened to,
where the only smell is
that of fire and ash.
A zone where battles are fought
but none fall dead -

The dead remaining alive
like zombies.
Thoughts roam relentlessly -
along with monsters in the mind,
that come to celebrate death
in noisy silence!
Where is this zone?
so well known
just by being unknown!

(09.08.2022)

* * * *

Tiny Treasures

The clear dew-drop on a leaf,
The moth in its flight so brief,
The ladybird with spotted wings,
The tiny humming bird that sings.
The firefly's gentle light,
The chirping crickets at night.
The small, wild flowers and sea shells,
The Baby's Breath and Blue Bells.
The little, busy bee, with great delight,
Pollinating the flowers in day light.
The intricate web a spider weaves,
The delicate lines on tiny leaves.
A feather floating in the air -
Presenting magic beyond compare!
A ray of sunshine and the moon light,
The sparkling stars in the sky at night.
A cool whispering sea breeze -
In all these we see God's expertise!

So, take a moment, slow down and see,
Such tiny treasures – so full, so free!

(25.09.2005)

* * * * *

To Know?

The unknown whispers of the night,
A presence felt, but never seen
A veil of intrigue, hiding from the light,
A mystery that dances in between
Dreams, beckoning with a silent call
To step in, to step out, to rise or fall,
To know the unknown is to know,
That there is still so much more to know!

(05.03.2024)

* * * *

Transient

As all burnt down in the fire's blaze,
And the ashes flew in muted haze,
All that once stood tall and strong,
Now to dust and shadows did belong.

In the fire the past flew in the breeze,
Ashes of memories lost in the leaves,
A plain reminder that life's so transient -
Each one is but a passing participant!

In the end we are left with dust and ashes,
With the passing of time – the past rehashes!

(26.12.2023)

* * * * *

Twinkle, Twinkle

Twinkle, twinkle solitary star
So alone and - oh so far!
In the dark of the night,
Anxious and so full of fright.

With joy this song is always sung,
How the little star up there is hung,
But don't you see the lonesome light,
Anxiously trying to shine so bright?

In the dark world that surrounds it,
Competing constantly to be fit,
This is surely not a pretty sight
As joyously children oft recite!

Twinkle, twinkle little star,
Now I wonder not what you are,
Just a lonely light up above,
Fighting to shine - with a push or shove!

Like the humans here below,
Wanting to do the best and glow!
Better than the best is best,
Leaving behind all who 'fail' this test!

Is this the shining star we, see
Twinkling up above to max degree?

(27.03.2011)

* * * *

Unfair

The caterpillar does all the work
Yet is despised;
The butterfly fluttering around
Gets so patronized.
A caterpillar's struggle – a story untold,
When the butterfly emerges so very bold!
In reality both are the same
Does one not see the end game?
Life is so unfair!
Oh, but do we care?
It happens all the time
And no one cares a dime!

(16.06.2003)

* * * * *

Unicorns in a Genocide

History records haunting tales,
Of genocide and colonization's trails,
The annals of how humans fail.
Leaving scars that time can't unveil.

Genocide - a word that chills the soul,
Where the powerful take complete control!
Innocents caught in hell hole's grip,
Their stories of horror make a tragic script.

Occupation – a conquest's cruel might -
Usurping lands, though it is not right,
Imposing power indoctrinated by fright,
Thus, erasing cultures, as identities take flight.

Oh, but in this milieu of politics and greed,
Sanctimonious rhetoric and crazy creed -
Let us all pretend, that we have agreed
That unicorns exist – oh yes, they do indeed!!!!

(03.04.2023)

* * * * *

Unvanquished

So often snipped in the bud,
Not allowed to take form and grow,
And when the snipping is not done,
Then the growth is orchestrated to be slow,
For want of proper food and nourishment.
In spite of this,
If growth does take place,
Then obstacles and impediments
Are placed, in this life's race.
Yet if the race is won,
By assiduousness and strife,
What awaits this tragic life,
Is but an awful sacrifice,
At the altar of selfishness and greed
This life? – 'tis indeed
That of the woman in our society.
Who is bound by stereotypical conformity!
But amidst all odds,
She stands unbeaten –

For down the ages,
She continues to persevere,
In this toxic social atmosphere

(16.08.1992)

* * * *

Utility of Negatives

If there's no night,
We will see no stars,
Freedom is in sight
Only through prison bars!

With no trial
We'll know no comfort,
Success is obtained
By tedious effort.

Only from filth
The lotus adorns its face,
Only through fire,
Does gold acquire its grace!

Recognize that
Grief adds to beauty,
Music is sweetest
In major and minor key!

Diamonds were but
Coal, under a mine
But when compressed and
Heated, they obtained their shine.

Joy and sorrow
Will make life complete,
Roses always grow
With cruel thorns at their feet!

(30.05.2004)

* * * * *

Veblen Was Right

In simplicity true beauty finds grace,
Conspicuous consumption is a damn disgrace!
Showy displays will only inflate
Pride, destroying one's peaceful state.

Veblen, your observation and keen insight,
Judged people and their pitiful plight!
Living up to the Joneses – a competitive strife,
Why not embrace a calmer life?

Give up the noise, the clatter, the race,
A simpler life will find a soothing space,
For in such humility, elegance finds a way,
Allowing beauty to permanently stay.

Watch the quiet flowers dance in glee,
Meek petals unfolding, for all to see,
From daisies to roses a colourful display!
No competition - each bloom has its own say.

The snail steadily moves at its own pace,
Never competing – simply finding its space -
A humble traveller leaving its mark behind,
A steady backpacker - peace it finds!

Nature has simplicity so profound,
One just needs to quietly look around!

(26.09.2019)

* * * * *

Void

Answering the call,
hearing the shell fall,
waves crashing like a tide -
hoping for solace to abide,
but the news stays to sting,
as echoes of loss persist to ring,
the void left cannot be filled -
as lingering memories are distilled.

(26.12.2019)

* * * * *

Wait

Patiently watch
with eyes open wide,
the world around transforms,
with each passing stride.
Nature's art work,
unfolds in rhyme,
in the zone of waiting,
with the symphony of time.

Like the caterpillar in the cocoon,
all hidden from view,
undergoes changes,
resulting in a vibrant hue,
as in this stillness,
a miracle takes form,
as out emerges the butterfly,
so vibrant and warm!

The tiny buds
bloom and unfurl,
splashing their colours,
in a riotous swirl.

So let us wait.
and do not stress,
for we will notice,
life will progress.

In the tapestry of time,
patience gently weaves,
it is better to surrender,
and all stress release,
watching life's wonders,
Delivering perfect peace!

(16.09.2007)

* * * *

What Matters

In the huge expanse of time and space,
We meander through this earthly place,
Seeking meaning in this world so vast -
Yet finding a void that seems to last.

We build our castles so colossal and grand,
Only to see them crumble as sand,
We chase after dreams that fade away,
Leaving us lost in the disarray.

The sun will rise and the sun will set,
What do we actually want to get?
In this grand scheme we are but a little speck,
Lost in this chaotic sea – a mere shipwreck.

Yet amidst all this futility there lies a spark,
A glimmer of hope, in this deepening dangerous dark,
When through it all we often find,
A thought, a dream, a promise all intertwined.

In spite of our transient world of futility,
We find ethereal beauty in our frailty
As against the shadows of our doubts, our dreams reappear
And all our worries, qualms and fears just disappear!

For in the end when all is said and done,
It is the journey that truly matters, not the outcome!

(07.11.2023)

* * * *

Where Are the Good Samaritans?

Where are the Good Samaritans
Of the world today?
People need their help,
Along life's by way.
Robbed, stripped, and wounded,
They lie there all day!
Where are the Good Samaritans,
Who will their pain allay?
Abused children, and women,
All cry out in need.
The old and the weak,
For assistance plead.
Wars and guns and nuclear bombs,
Wiping life away,
Where are the Good Samaritans
Of the world today?

(18.08.1993)

* * * * *

Who Said We Women Can't?

Break the glass ceilings,
Release our dreams and feelings,
That we have forever kept locked,
As routes for us have been blocked,
When they say women can't!

Let's smash our glass shoes,
And walk free sans blues,
Break out of the golden cage,
Challenge systemic societal rage,
Who said we women can't?

Shatter traditional barriers – never fret,
We can rise above all limits they have set
For us, and with courage pave our way,
Creating a brighter future, a freer day.
Who said we women can't?

Our talents are exponential,
Our fortitude exceptional,

We do have immense potential,
Hence, we women can!

(08.03.2024)

* * * * *

Will He Not Care?

When God has made this great big earth,
Has planned the wonders of my birth,
Will He not care for me?

When He has flung this earth in space,
Spinning it at a given pace,
Does He not care for me?

When God forms the sun's golden rays,
Setting it up with its warm blaze,
Will He not care for me?

When He places the moon on high,
Like a silver disc, in the night sky,
Will He not care for me?

When God pins each star above,
As a symbol of His abiding love,
Can He then not care for me?

When He cares for sparrows small,
Numbering when each of them fall,
Will He not care for me?

When he paints each insect's wing,
Creates music for every bird to sing,
Will he not then care for me?

His creation's intricate design,
Is a reflection of His love divine,
And a testament, that He surely cares for me!

(12.11.1999)

* * * * *

You Tried

You tried to destroy
myself in me,
you tried to steal
my identity.

You say I have contempt,
since you failed in your attempt,
to break me, and tear me apart,
but you only strengthen
the will in my heart.
For I am resilient,
as from the start,
I know all your deception
and obfuscation
will fail, for I find the truth!
As amidst the misconception,
I remain resolute.

In the shadows of doubt,
I will always find light,

And with courage,
I will continue to fight!

(29.09.2016)

* * * *

Synopsis

It is indeed a fascination how our thoughts can lead us on to an expedition through the landscapes of our minds, so much like the hiker's navigation through assorted uncharted territories. Each thought no matter how strange, outlandish and bizarre contributes to the tapestry of our very being - unlocking the mysteries of life. As one continues to traverse the trails of thought delving into the nuances, intricacies and convolutions of human experiences with their biases, emotions and passions, one is bound to uncover new insights and perspectives. The poems in this book are a reflection of the author's profound explorations which at times are lateral in interpretation, but capture the essence of life's complications in a unique and unexpected way. The poetic journeys in this book are a testament to the beauty of chaos and complexity of the human mind.

About the Author

Crystal David John, a Ph.D. in Economics, is a strong feminist and an active advocate of gender justice. A distinguished scholar and beloved teacher, writer, artist and poet she has dedicated her lifetime to the pursuit of knowledge. Her stories, cryptic comments and stimulating classroom lessons, all the time encouraging students to think and be original - have always made her a favourite among her students and friends. Her one-of-a-kind teaching, elusive sarcasm, exclusive sense of humour combined with concern and compassion appealed to students from all walks of life.

The poetry she has compiled in this book - "Trails of Thought" powerfully captures her distinct outlook on life. The diverse range of perspectives presented in this book is both unmatched and characteristic of her individual style and approach to life. Through her poems, Crystal leaves behind a lasting legacy as an educator, mentor, advisor, confidante, loyal companion, ruthless critic, keen observer of humanity, and wellspring of motivation.